The Ghosts of Henry VIII

Written By

Keith Coy

The Ghosts of Henry VIII

Table of Contents

Dedication 2

I. 1

Winter, 1546. 1

II. 18

III. 31

IV. 41

V. 51

VI. 62

January 1547 62

VII. 70

VIII. 75

IX. 80

27th/28th January 1547. 80

Keith Coy

Dedication

I would like to dedicate my book to my mum Collette Coy and my fellow ghost enthusiasts Zoe Gavin and Mary Jenner.

The Ghosts of Henry VIII

I.

Winter, 1546.

Henry VIII had been King of England for over thirty seven years. His reign had seen many turbulent events; six different marriages from Catherine of Aragon who truly loved him to Catherine Parr who he saw as a nurse maid. Many different mistresses, the birth of three; two of whom he sadly lost. The birth of two daughters; both of whom he removed from and instated to the line of succession. The rise and fall of many advisors including Thomas Cromwell. The shock executions of friends such as Sir Thomas More and two wives. And the shocking break with the Church of Rome.

This winter, however, saw any event that not only did many Tudor courtiers do their very best to keep from being discovered but terrified

Keith Coy

them. An event that many would have forgotten about. Not only was this winter to be Henry VIII's last; it was to be the winter that the Tudor King was haunted… By ghosts!

Snow covered the land in a thick white blanket. The heavy grey sky hung above ready to let more snow fall at any time. Every field and hedge was covered. In London, the river Thames was completely frozen solid with thick ice. People had gathered on the frozen river and merchants had set up stalls to sell their wares. The sound of people talking and music filled the air. A priest walked along the river with a small wooden box in one hand and ringing a bell with the other hand. "Let us pray, remember those less fortunate than us at this time of the year!" Said the priest. A young man placed a few coins into the box "Thank you sir, blessings of the day to you!"

A cloth merchant on his stall was busy trying to convince someone

The Ghosts of Henry VIII

to buy some of his cloth. "I assure you sir, this is finest of cloth. Worn only by those at court. Fifty five shillings." He said as he unravelled the roll of cloth. " If not, then I can recommend this." He pulled out a roll of cloth of blue with yellow and gold thread interwoven in it. "As worn by the Lady Anne of Cleves herself. Perfect for lady wife. Sixty shillings." He said. At the next stall, a young woman was selling baskets and on another stall, an elderly gent was selling bread and bread rolls.

A butcher was standing outside his stall, trying to attract some customers. "I have the finest meats here this day," said the butcher, "I have beef, pork, mutton, lamb, chicken, and fowl." A woman walked past. "I have rabbit, hare, fish and just for this time of year; goose. Come and see what meat you fancy for your dinner tables." A large group of children ran and slid across the ice, much to the annoyance of many people. They passed the pie stall where a

Keith Coy

tall boy swiped a large tray of pies and they all ran off. "Oi! You cheeky little urchins," Called the pie man, "Come back with those pies" The children all took a pie and placed it in their mouths. The pie man let out a hearty laugh. "Ok then go on, have those on me."

Nearly by there were other things going on as well. On the river banks was a game of football. A couple of men were practising their archery skills. A horse race was taking place with people place bets and cheering on the horses. It really was your typical average Tudor winter day. There were even people crossing the frozen river with carts, hoping that the ice wouldn't crack or break under the weight. Musicians played many different tunes on their many instruments and a chorus of people were singing.

Outside of Whitehall Palace, in the stables, the workers went about their usual day to day activities. Some were grooming the horses, some

The Ghosts of Henry VIII

were cleaning out the stables. A couple of sweepers swept some water along the cobbles in the courtyard. Up in the hay loft, a worker caught a bale of hay that was thrown up to him. "Ok, not bad but come over to me a bit with the next one." He said as he put the bale into the loft. The worker below him picker up another bale and threw it up to the other worker who caught it. "Good." He said. The worker put the bale into the loft. He turned round and was surprised to see what looked like a snowman walking towards the loft. It stopped and shook all the snow off of itself to reveal a man underneath with a bright red nose. "Damn it Andrew!" Shouted the worker, "Get inside and warm thyself by the fire now!"

There was a fair amount of activity at the palace itself. As the sun began to set, workers started to finish up their work in the courtyards. The courtyard where the under croft was located saw workers rolling barrels in and out of the cellars. Men rolled wooden trollies into sheds while others carried crates into the palace. A steward watched as the last of the workers finished up. "Right, close the gates!" the steward shouted across the courtyard. Two guards closed the gates which sounded with loud bang like thunder throughout the area. The steward nodded, turned round and headed inside.

In the next courtyard, more workers were busy packing away their tools and other equipment like ladders. A few women walked across the courtyard carrying baskets. They turned a corner and headed down a cloister and entered the kitchen courtyard. In this courtyard were men pulling carts and trollies. The women placed the baskets next to some other women who were busy plucking birds and getting them ready to be taken into the kitchens. There were small burners with fires lit all around the courtyard.

The Ghosts of Henry VIII

In the Butchery, the butchers were busy preparing the meats for the different dishes in the other vast kitchens. The prepared meats were taken off while the unprepared meats were brought in. One butcher picked up a knife and began sharpening it on a stone pedal wheel before he turned and began to skin a hare on a table next to him.

In the boiling house, workers and cooks were hard at work getting all the soups and broths ready. One worker went up to the large boiling pot where he picked up a large ladle, plunged it into the pot and pulled out a large spoon full of cooked meat. He placed the meat into a bucket on the side next to him and plunged the ladle into the pot again. Once the bucket was full, he took it to a nearby work bench where another worker started placing the meat into pie casings.

A steward entered the boiling house and a young cook leaned over the wooden railing with a spoon. The steward tasted the soup on the spoon. "Very good." He said, "It needs a little more salt. Remember now, this is all going up to the great hall so we want them to be able to taste it." The young cook nodded and returned to his cooking pot where he added a pinch or two of salt to the soup and stirred it. The steward went over to check on the other workers.

In the fish kitchen, the cooks prepared all the fish dishes. There was a smoker where salmon, trout and haddock were being smoked. On a nearby work table, a cook was adding the final touches to a finished dish. In the bake house, the bakers were hard at work getting all the bread rolls ready and taken off to the tables upstairs. In the confectionery, all the sweet dishes and table decorations were being made. Sugar cards and marzipan chessboards. Fruit pies and sugar tarts sat cooling, waiting to be taken to the great hall.

The Ghosts of Henry VIII

In the grand kitchen, the spits were blazing with large roaring fires and all the meats cooking. The steward entered and was pleased with how everything. Then he spotted the centrepiece for the King's table still sitting by the serving hatch. He quickly ordered two men to help him take it upstairs.

Up in the great hall, the atmosphere was very different. The hall was beautifully decorated with colourful paper chains and holly wreaths. Garlands adorned the walls and the minstrels' gallery. Tables had been laid out around the hall with red and green cloth as well as the food that been brought up from the kitchens already. The kitchen steward and his men placed the centrepiece onto a table next to a raised platform before heading back downstairs.

On the raised platform was a canopy of purple cloth with the royal coat of arms embroidered with gold thread on it. Under the canopy sat the royal family. Henry VIII sat in the centre with his son Prince Edward on his knee while his wife Catherine Parr and his youngest daughter Elizabeth sat to his left. On his right sat his eldest daughter Mary and his ex-wife turned sister Anne of Cleves. Outside of the canopy sat the infamous brothers, Edward and Thomas Seymour.

Henry gave Prince Edward to Catherine, got up and moved forward. Everyone in the hall bowed and the music stopped. "I bid you all welcome," Henry said, "To my Christmas party here at Whitehall Palace!" Everyone began to applaud. "As you know, the festive time will soon be upon us. So I command you to enjoy thyselves!" Everyone cheered as Henry sat down again. The music played again and a couple singing minstrels stepped forward and sang pastime with good company.

As the party got into full swing, people began to enjoy themselves whilst others talked about the recent downfall of the notorious Duke of Norfolk.

"I thought he was never going to get what he deserves!"

"Agreed! What kind of man could do what he has done and to members of his own family."

"Well, I will certainly be in the front of the crowd when he takes to the scaffolding."

"See where greed gets you? I mean look what he did to poor Thomas Cromwell"

"I hope the axe is blunt and he suffers terribly!"

The singing minstrels then began to sing greensleeves and people started dancing. A couple of jesters entered the hall and made people laugh with antics and high jinks. It was going to be a good night or so people thought.

Keith Coy

As the sun outside disappeared for the night and the moon shone through the windows, stewards set about lighting candles and chandeliers along with extra fires to allow the festivities to continue. The food was slowly being eaten with more dishes and plates being brought up. Wine, ale and beer was being drunk in good quantity and everyone bid goodnight to Prince Edward as the party went long into the night.

Everything seemed to be going well and Henry relaxed. But like with a lot of things, if it was going well then it was too good to be true and this was certainly the case. Then it happened.

Out of nowhere, a sudden gust of wind appeared. Blowing up such a gale. Hats and hoods were blown off. The tapestries banged against the walls. The flames of the candles and fires flickered and dimed as if they were about to go out. The table cloths flapped about and the bottles and goblets on the tables were

The Ghosts of Henry VIII

knocked over with some rolling to the floor. The canopy rocked as Elizabeth clung to Catherine while both Anne and Mary struggled to hold onto their hoods. Henry looked around with anger in his eyes at the commotion that was taking place. The Seymour brothers were sent flying across the hall away from the canopy and crashing into the wall behind them. People looked around in shock, many were struggling to stay on the feet against the strong wind that decimating the hall. The minstrels stepped back, some falling over as a large tapestry flapped up towards them. The windows shook and rattled against the wind. Then suddenly and as mysteriously as it had started. The wind stopped.

The hall was a mess. Stillness gripped the room. The paper chains and garlands hanged half off the walls and holly wreaths fell to the floor with a crash. The courtiers were stunned and looked around with the royal family in shock and confusion. What had just happened?

"Someone check the doors now!" demanded a very angry Henry. A guard left the great hall and come back again. "They are closed Your Majesty!" Henry's eyes widened.

Catherine quickly stood up, her hat now on the floor. "Let us resume the festivities and forget about what has just occurred. She said motioning to the minstrels who began to play again. Catherine sat down again. "Come Henry, let us not allow this to ruin a good night." Henry nodded. "Yes, you are right my Queen." The courtiers nervously continued the party, unable to ignore the event that just happened.

Henry looked out at the hall before turning and seeing the Seymours picking themselves up off the floor. Something wasn't right and Henry knew it. As he turned his gaze back into the hall and onto the court again. He spotted something that made him flinch and the colour drain from his face.

The Ghosts of Henry VIII

Amongst the many courtiers, was a face that Henry hadn't seen since 1529. The face was that of his friend and former mentor Cardinal Thomas Wolsey. Wolsey stood there among the court as he still belonged there, just staring at Henry with an icy stare. A red glow was emanating around him. He had a pale face with pale hands except for two large red dots on one hand. His red cardinal robes which were once bright red now looked dull and his large gold and ruby crucifix hung around his neck like it had been in life except now it was pale in comparison to its former opulence. Henry swallowed and struggled to his feet nearly knocking his walking staff over as he did. Everyone turned around.

Henry never took his stare off of Wolsey who continued to stare back coldly. "What do you want?!" Demanded Henry, "Why have you come back?!" People began to look around, some murmured even whispering to each other. Henry staggered a bit, becoming unsteady on his weak legs and barely able to hold onto his staff, prompting both Catherine and Anne to get up and hold him steady. They both looked at each other with looks of worry and concern on their faces.

"Will you not speak to me?" Shrieked Henry in desperation but Wolsey just stared chillingly at the frail King. "If it is forgiveness you seek then you have it. If it is my apology you want then I am sorry!" Henry said with a tremble in his voice. Mary looked over at Elizabeth who was looking scared by their father's strange outbursts. People began to get nervous with some backing away from the raised platform. Edward Seymour went to move forward but was stopped by Thomas.

Then after a few moments of Wolsey just standing there and staring; he raised one of his pale hands, pointed at Henry and let out eerily one word:

"Tudor!"

The Ghosts of Henry VIII

This sound could only be heard by Henry and it emanated with such a low pitch that Henry's eyes widened with fear. The colour completely drained from his face. Then he let out a very loud scream in terror making people jump. Mary jumped to her feet but Anne raised her hand to stop Mary from approaching Henry.

Catherine went white in the face herself unable to bring herself to terms with what has just happened. Henry was still staring out at the hall and was now trembling. "My Lords and Ladies, it is with great regret that the hour has grown late and the King is very tired." She said, "Please let us all turn in for the night." People began to exit the great hall; Catherine motioned to the guards to help Henry. Henry thanked her for her support. Just as he was about to leave the hall, he looked back at where Wolsey was standing but he was gone and there was nothing there but an empty space.

II.

The next day, the snow blew about in the wind and laid even thicker on the ground. Inside the palace, workers were busy going about their day as usual. Hard at work getting the palace ready for Christmas. In the great hall stood Archbishop Thomas Cranmer, looking around at the state of the room before him. Catherine Parr had ordered that the hall was not to be touched until she said otherwise so the archbishop could have a good look. He shook his head as he tried to figure out what happened the night before.

A door opened and Bishop Stephen Gardiner entered. "Stephen," Thomas said, shaking his companion's hand. "Thank you for coming." Stephen nodded. "I see what you mean." Stephen said, looking around. "What do you think could have happened here last night?" Thomas moved closer to Stephen taking care not to be overheard. "Well from what I have been told; the King saw someone or something." Stephen looked stunned. Thomas pointed to the canopy. "Let's go over there."

The two bishops moved to the canopy and stood on the raised platform, both looking out into the hall. "It must have been somewhere around the middle of the hall." Said Thomas pointing out into the hall. Stephen struggled with what he heard. "I cannot understand what could have happened!" He said as he scanned the hall, "Could this be the work of some ill-fated jester?" Thomas shook his head. "I have no idea!"

Thomas looked around to see if anyone was around or listening to them before turning back to Stephen. "From what I have been told, a mysterious bout of wind stirred up and caused a great gale." Stephen was shocked to hear this but before he could speak there as a loud bang as if a door nearby slammed shut. The two bishops stepped down from the platform, moved away from the canopy and headed out of the great hall.

"Are you trying to tell me that something unnatural did occur last night?" Asked Stephen as the bishops made their way down a gallery. Thomas shook his head, "I know not what happened last night but I am told that the King did let out such a scream that it caught everyone by surprise and made them all jump."

The bishops turned a corner and entered a plain looking room. This room was not as lavish or as beautiful as the other rooms for this was the scribes' room. There were only three desks in the room all adorned with parchments, quills and ink bottles. There were small bits of parchment littered on the floor and a small fire lit in the corner of the room. Thomas went to the nearest desk and sat down on a chair. Stephen sat on a chair near the door. "What are you going to do?" Stephen asked. Thomas rubbed his eyes. "I know not." He said warily. Just as Stephen was

The Ghosts of Henry VIII

about to say something else, a page entered the room. "Here you are, Your Grace!" The page said. Thomas let out a sorrowful sigh.

"What is it? What do you want?" Asked Thomas as the page bowed. "The King has commanded that you attend him at once." Said the page. Thomas jumped to his feet. "I am coming now!" He said and he raced out of the room completely forgetting about Stephen who was taken by surprise at what had just happened. "Wait for me!" He cried.

Stephen made his way towards the chapel alone, looking around to see if he could spot the archbishop along the way but to no avail. He turned into the cloister and stared down at it. The cloister seemed different for some reason. He was staring into a strange darkness which was unusual. Stephen felt uneasy. A shadow crept along the cobbled ground towards him. Then halfway down the cloister, a mysterious white light shone and the silhouette of a lady appeared wearing a gable hood. Stephen stared for a moment. "Can I help you madam?" Stephen asked but a door slamming made him jump. After looking around to see if anyone was coming, he was shocked to turn round again and see that the lady and the darkness were gone.

"Here you are!" Thomas said as he came round the corner. "Come, the King awaits!" Then he spotted the confused look on Stephen's face. "What is it? What is wrong?" He asked. Stephen looked around. "Did you see where the lady went?" He asked. Thomas shook his head. "I saw no lady here, only you. Come, the King awaits!" He said.

The two bishops made their way through the palace via the many corridors and galleries. People bowed and curtsied as they passed by. One man even stopped them briefly to ask for their blessings, which they gave. Then they came across a door with a guard standing outside it. "Halt, why do you approach the King's privy apartment stairs?" The guard demanded. Thomas stepped forward. "We are about the King's business and we have been summoned before the King." He said without wasting any time. The guard stiffened up. "Identify yourselves at once. Nobody may pass without identifying themselves first." He said roughly. Thomas tutted. "You Sir, are an idiot!" He said with frustration in his voice. The guard straightened his halberd. "No one may enter the King's privy apartments without identifying themselves."

Stephen stepped forward. "My good man, are so you duty bound to the King that you do not see standing before you, the Archbishop of Canterbury; Dr Thomas Cranmer or myself Bishop Stephen Gardiner?" He asked as the guard tried to stiffen up some more but went bright red with embarrassment. "I am sorry, Your Graces, but you know the King's command." He said, stepping aside and opening the door. Thomas let out a small growl. "That could very well cost you your immortal soul." The guard gulped. Stephen thanked the guard and the two bishops entered through the door.

Beyond the door was a very large staircase which was split into three sections. On top of the first section sat a yeoman. He stood up. "What brings you to the King's privy apartments, Your Graces?" He asked. "The King's business!" replied Thomas. The yeoman beckoned them forward. Thomas and Stephen climbed the first section of the stairs. "I must ask that you leave any and all defenses here," The yeoman said, "From this moment until you leave the King's apartments, you are now under the protection of my men." After realizing that he was talking to two bishops and apologizing, the yeoman escorted them to the top section of the staircase where two large wooden doors sat. "If you would like to wait here I shall inform His Majesty's secretary that you are here." The yeoman said and he entered through the doors

The Ghosts of Henry VIII

As they waited, Stephen told Thomas about what he saw earlier. The strange darkness, the shadow on the cobbles and the mysterious white light. Thomas shook his head. "It makes no sense, why are things happening?" Thomas said. Stephen looked down the staircase to make sure they were alone. "I have no idea. Yet in that white light, I did spy a lady in a gable hood." He said. Thomas snapped his head up a bit. "Who was she?" He asked with slight interest. Stephen looked back at Thomas, "I know not, for I only glanced at her for a moment before I was distracted by a door slamming."

Before Thomas could enquire some more, the doors opened and the yeoman stepped out. "Ok, Your Graces, you may enter." Said the yeoman as he descended the stairs back to his desk. The bishops entered the room. This room was dull with only drapes on the walls, a few awful paintings and a small fire lit at the back. The King's secretary moved forward. "The King will see you now, he is in his privy dining room" He said. The bishops thanked the secretary who motioned to a guard to escort them through the adjacent rooms.

As they passed through the many and vast rooms, they were overwhelmed by the sizes of each room and the colours and furnishings that sat in them. They even passed through the King's office and the waiting area where the famous Whitehall Mural was located. They then descended down a small staircase and round a corner. They were then taken into the King's private library. Here they stopped for a few minutes. "If you would like to wait here, the King will send for you shortly." The guard said.

After a brief wait, a bell sounded and a small door in the corner opened. "Come in here now!" Called Henry with his usual anger. Thomas and Stephen entered into the King's private dining room. Inside this room was very different to the public dining room. The walls were decorated with gold and silver drapes

The Ghosts of Henry VIII

and small tapestries. There were three small windows. Two plain glass and one stained glass. There were also portraits on the walls. On one wall were the portraits of Henry VII, Elizabeth of York, Lady Margaret Beaufort and Prince Arthur. On another wall were portraits of Catherine of Aragon , Sir Thomas More and Sir Thomas Cromwell. On an easel sat the portrait of Jane Seymour. In front of this portrait was a small medium table with food on it and sat behind the table was Henry himself. There was a medium fireplace opposite the table with a roaring fire lit inside it. Just above the fireplace sat the portrait of Cardinal Wolsey.

"Do not just stand there damn it," Snapped Henry. "Sit you both down!" Thomas and Stephen walked up to the table and bowed. "Never mind all that, sit you both down!" Both bishops pulled up a chair and sat down at the table. The small door closed. "Help yourself to some food." Henry said. Stephen picked up a roll while Thomas helped himself to some grapes. "I take you heard about last night?" Henry said sulkily. Thomas nodded, "Yes sire and can I say I do not believe a word of it?" Henry glared at him. "No you may not." He snapped, "It is all true. I was made to look like a fool and I will not have." Stephen placed the roll onto a small plate. "You think that someone was having you on, Majesty?" He asked. Henry glared at him too. "Eat that roll, I am not having you waste my food. And I do not think it, I know it!"

Thomas finished the grapes he was eating and looked at Stephen and then at Henry. "I wonder, Your Majesty, if maybe that someone has decided that you needed to be reminded of what has happened in the past. And given how close to the late cardinal you were, they thought it best.." Henry started his usual angered snarling. "Then I suggest that you investigate this matter immediately." He said picking up a roll and breaking it into two halves. "I want the person or people involved

The Ghosts of Henry VIII

in this to feel the full force of my anger! Remind them of the soon to be former Duke of Norfolk."

Thomas nodded though he was trembling slightly. "I will do my very best to find those involved and bring them to justice in your name." He said. Henry took a bite of one of the rolls. "See that you do." He said, dismissing the bishops with his free hand. Thomas and Stephen got up and bowed before backing away from the table. The small door opened again and they both turned and exited the dining room. Back in the library again, Stephen let out a small sigh of relief. "We will need to work twice as hard than usual to solve this one." He said just as the yeoman reappeared and proceeded to escort them out the private apartments.

Back in the dining room, Henry sulkily ate his roll now that he was alone again. He looked around the room to see if he could find a servant to attend him but there was no one around. He then looked up at the portrait of Wolsey above the fireplace. Henry dropped the roll that he was eating and fear gripped him. His eyes widened with fright as he watched the sight before. The portrait of Wolsey began to move. The figure lowered his fingers and hand in the painting and turned his head to face Henry. There was such anger in his expressions. Then the eerie sound from the night before echoed. "Tudor!" Henry tried to call out but he was too frightened, he couldn't even let out a cry. Wolsey's portrait continued to turn. Henry closed his eyes for a few seconds and when he opened them again, everything and the portrait was back to normal. Henry began to gasp for air.

III.

A couple of days later and things in Whitehall Palace were now very uncomfortable and very awkward. Henry refused to leave his apartments and so Mary had to attend to matters of state like going to Privy Council meetings while Catherine held audiences on Henry's behalf. It just seemed normal, nothing unusual. That is until one afternoon.

Henry made a rare public appearance to reassure his courtiers that he was fine and that there was nothing to worry about. Henry, Catherine and Mary made their way to the public dining hall where it was tradition, in cases where the monarch hasn't seen for days, for the royal house to have a meal in front of the court. Anne, Elizabeth and Edward were already in the room and waiting for Henry to arrive. When they entered the room, everyone bowed and curtsied while a small fanfare played. Henry took his seat at the centre of the table while Catherine sat next to him and Mary sat next to Edward. A meal had been prepared and brought up. A variety of meats, pies, bread rolls and other dishes laid out on the table with a large peacock centrepiece adorned the table.

    "Let us give thanks for this fine feast." Said Henry as Thomas stepped forward. Everyone said a quick prayer with the royal family before they sat down. Everyone on the table washed their hands and then tucked into the meal. "Mary, I hear you have been attending my affairs." Henry said, turning to his eldest. Mary nodded, "Yes father and there are a few issues you be made aware of." She said but Henry shook his head. "No, whatever they might be, I have faith that you will deal them." Mary looked deflated but composed her gracefully and picked up a small piece of chicken. "Very well, as you wish father." The topic was quickly changed and the meal went splendidly. That was until Henry looked up from the table and spotted something in the back corner of the room. Standing there in a purple dress and a gable hood was his first wife Catherine of Aragon. Her once beautiful features had now faded and she was very pale in the face except for one feature. From her eyes and down her cheeks were what looked like tear tracks only it looked like they were made with blood.

Henry gasped aloud, making everyone jump. Mary tutted. "Not again father, what is it this time?" Henry turned to Mary and pointed to the corner. "Your mother is standing there. Look, do you not see her?!" He cried. Mary looked to the corner where Henry was pointing but it was empty. Mary became very angry. "Father, if this is some kind of jest then it is not funny. How dare you say such a thing." Mary threw her cloth onto the table, got up and stormed out. Anne got up too. "I will go after her." She said and headed out the same way Mary did. Henry looked shocked and returned his gaze back to the corner. Catherine of Aragon was still standing there.

"Can no one see her standing there?" He said with a tremble in his voice. Catherine Parr got slightly annoyed. "Henry, will you stop this? You are frightening Elizabeth and Edward." Then she got up and made for the door followed by the prince and Elizabeth. The small crowd also left except for Thomas who was now looking at the corner. "Are you sure that you are seeing Catherine of Aragon?" He asked. Henry stood up, grabbed Thomas, turned him around and pressed his face Thomas' "Are you calling me a liar?" He said. Thomas gulped. "Well no Your Majesty." Henry let Thomas go. "Good. I know what I am seeing."

Henry and Thomas left the dining room and headed for Henry's private apartments. Along the way, they met up with Stephen. Thomas told Stephen about what happened in the dining room. Stephen was stunned. Neither priest knew what was happening and

The Ghosts of Henry VIII

what was worse, the King's public outbursts were becoming the main topic for gossip amongst the courtiers. Not just the Upper court but the lower court as well including the servants.

Once in the private apartments, Henry sent for a pitcher of ale while Thomas and Stephen sat down next to the fire. "How is the investigation faring?" Asked Henry as he sat down next to the fire as well, placing his leg on a small stall. Thomas looked at Stephen who was staring into the fire. "Well sire, it seems that nobody is willing to come forth and admit they are responsible for the night of the party, so I am afraid that the investigation is going nowhere." He said. Henry placed his staff against the wall next to the fireplace. "Well you better find some answers soon. It is nearly Christmas and I will not have the yuletide ruined by this. And I want you to find out who that was in the public dining room. I will not be embarrassed like that!"

Keith Coy

After a while and a few goblets of ale, Henry fell asleep in his chair so the two priests saw themselves out, being careful not to make any noise and risk the King's anger. The winter sun faded and slowly turned to darkness outside. The room seemed still and peaceful with the gentle crackling of the now low fire. Henry must have felt a slight chill as he shook himself awake. The room was dimly lit and as he was about to call for some candles to be lit, he spotted Catherine of Aragon standing in front of the chairs next to the fire.

The fire lit her pale face exposing the blood like tear tracks on her cheeks. Henry tried to speak but he was gripped with fear. Catherine stared at him for a few seconds. "Look what has become of me," She said with coldness in her voice, "Look what you have become responsible for." Henry splattered a bit but still no words came out. Catherine stepped forward. "Henry, you have angered a lot of beings with

The Ghosts of Henry VIII

your actions over the years. The jousting accident that you had right before I passed; was meant to be a warning but you just ignored it." Henry choked slightly before he finally spoke. "What is this of which you speak?" He asked gasping for air. "Why are you here?" Catherine leaned in slightly to Henry. "Hear me Henry, we are the first. There are others who will come. You are a sinner Henry and for this you must repent." Henry tried to stand up. After struggling for a few seconds, he grabbed his staff and got to his feet.

Henry moved away from the fire. "What do you mean, we are the first? Is that why Wolsey has come as well?" He asked without looking back. The hairs on his neck stood up which told him that Catherine had moved behind him. "Yes Wolsey has persuaded the powers above to allow us to come back and get you to change before you pass. Your soul has become a desired prize for the darkness. As I said, we are the first, others will come."

Keith Coy

Henry picked up a goblet and took a drink. His head was starting to spin. His first wife was standing in the room with him. He had not seen her since 1533 when he banished her from his court and sent her to Kimbolton Castle. He was having great difficulty taking in what she was saying. What did she mean that his soul was a desired prize for the darkness? Who were these others that were coming? None of this was making sense.

"I do not believe anything of which you speak!" He said with his usual viciousness. "I am not a prize for anyone. Now go and leave me!" Catherine stepped back. She raised her hands towards Henry. "In life, you did me wrong and broke the sanctity of your marriage vows and sent me away. You are in great danger and you must repent. I will stay until such time as you do!" She said as a bright white light began to emanate around her. Then she vanished right before Henry's eyes.

The Ghosts of Henry VIII

The door opened and a servant entered followed by Thomas and Stephen. " Are you ok Sire? Asked Thomas. Henry glared. "Yes, get this room lit now!" After a few minutes the room lit with dozens of candles. Henry waited for the servants to leave before he recounted his tale to the bishops. Thomas gulped as he remembered what had happened to Catherine of Aragon. "I remember all too well. I oversaw it all at your behest." He said. Henry scowled at him. Thomas backed off.

"I want this investigated and I want it investigated now!" Demanded Henry. The bishops bowed. "We will not rest until we know the truth." Stephen said. Henry told them both to leave and they did. Henry banged his staff on the ground.

"Now hear me Wolsey, Catherine and whoever else is here! I am not a sinner. My soul is not a desired prize, for the darkness or otherwise. I am the King. Supreme head of the Church of England. I am Henry VIII!"

Keith Coy

There was nothing but silence filled the room. Henry looked around but there was no one else there. He thought that he had gotten his word through. Henry then proceeded to make his way to his bedchamber. Then the air became unsettled. Henry felt a cold breeze around.

"Repent now before you pass!"

IV

A few days before Christmas, Henry refused to see anyone other than the priests. Only appearing in public to make announcements and speeches. Thomas began to suspect that the King was suffering a fever of the mind but he dared not speak of it to anyone, not even Stephen. It was like Henry was more erratic than usual.

Then one afternoon short of Christmas Eve, Henry called his family and the priests to his chambers. It was an uncomfortable and awkward meeting. Outside the window, the snow flurried around and a small robin flew up to the window and landed on the sill. Henry stared at the little bird before turning into the room. "I have summoned you all here for a reason. Catherine, my Queen; I am sending you and my children to Hampton Court Palace for Christmas. It will only be for a little while." Henry said as struggled over to a chair and sat down. Mary frowned; she didn't like what was happening to father as it was. "Oh I see how it is," She snarled, "Send us away so that you do not become tempted to think that we think you mad, is that it?"

Catherine was stunned, "How can you say that to your sovereign father?" She asked. Mary turned to her stepmother. "How can you think it is acceptable to have us sent away at this time when we should all be together.?" Henry lost his patience, "Enough!" He roared; "You are going to Hampton Court and that is the end of the matter. Now go!" Catherine, Mary and the children left. Henry little knowing that this was to be one of the last times that he would see his family again.

Once the others were out of the room, Henry turned to Anne of Cleves. "Anne, my beloved sister and devoted servant." He began. Anne burst into tears, "Oh Henry!" She sobbed. Henry comforted her. "Anne, come come now.

The Ghosts of Henry VIII

I want you to go with my family and have a wonderful Christmas." He said. At that moment, a strange whistling sound could be heard in the room. "What on Earth is that sound?" Asked Anne as everyone looked around.

Henry told Anne to catch up with the others and to have a good time over the festive period, Anne departed the room and Henry turned to Thomas and Stephen who were still looking confused by the sound they had heard before anyone could speak the strange whistle sounding again this time followed by "Harry!"

Henry's face went quite pale as he recognized the voice. It cannot be. No it cannot. The two priests looked at Henry who struggled slowly into his chair again. Stephen turned to Thomas to say something but he noticed that the archbishop had gone white himself. "Harry!" The voice sounded again. "Majesty, I think it is time that the good Doctor Cramner and I continued with our work." Stephen said and he made his way to the door. Thomas quickly followed, almost running out of the door.

As the afternoon slowly progressed to evening, Henry watched as the sleighs taking his family to Hampton Court Palace departed on the frozen river. He could hear the joyful tones of the people outside being merry. Henry gave a small smile to servants who were walking past and happened to notice him standing in the window and bowed.

Once the sleighs disappeared from view and the servants quickly moved along, Henry went and sat by the fire. He stared into the fire before looking up at a painting. It was nothing special or fancy, just a painting that Henry liked. Then after a few seconds, something began to happen. The ghostly image of Wolsey appeared and stared at the now terrified Henry. With a ghostly moan of sorts, Wolsey said; "Repent! You must repent!" before disappearing from the painting again. Henry struggled some breaths before

The Ghosts of Henry VIII

reaching for a goblet next to him and looking inside. "How potent is this wine?" He mumbled to himself.

The light outside the window began to fade and the servants lit a load of candles while food was being brought in and placed on a table next to the King. It seemed that the events of the afternoon had passed and that everything was going to be fine. Henry demanded to be left alone while he ate and said that he would call if he needed some assistance. Then once he was alone, he slowly tucked into a meal. He took a big swig of wine from his goblet and let out a very big burp. "Ah much delight!" He said.

"You always did enjoy your food Harry" Came a voice out of the shadows, "And your wine. But your food more. The size of all your kitchens." Henry slowly placed his goblet on the table and looked towards the area where the voice was coming from. "Whoever you are, better show thyself or I will call for my guard." He said. There was a small blast of cold air followed by a small gust of wind and then out of the shadows appeared the ghost of Henry's oldest friend, Sir Thomas More. Unlike Wolsey or Catherine of Aragon, his ghost appeared unchanged or unmarked. Henry's eyes widened as Thomas approached the table.

"Look all you want, Harry but you will not find a single blemish." Said Thomas stopping in front of Henry. "Though you think me marked after having my head removed, I bear you no ill will." Henry didn't know what to make of this. How is this happening? Then he looked at the wine. "This wine is too strong. Aye that be it. Too strong." He said and looked back at Thomas. "Aye and you are just a figment of a brewer's attempt to ruin a good King!" He pointed at Thomas who looked down at his once and former friend. "Aye, you are not really here, I have fallen asleep and this is a dream of sorts, a really bad.." The strangle whistle sounded again cutting Henry off.

The Ghosts of Henry VIII

"Believe what you like Harry but they are not pleased with you." Thomas said as he proceeded to take a seat opposite Henry. "You are being given a chance to save your mortal soul from the darkness. Why will you not take it?" Henry stuttered for a few seconds getting out words like soul and wine. Thomas looked at the spread on the table. "I remember the times you used to throw banquets just because you could. You could enjoy another banquet if you just repent." Henry quickly shook himself out of his stupor and glared at Thomas. "Repent?!" He snapped, "I am not a sinner nor am I a desired prize."

Thomas got up and walked back towards the shadows before stopping and turning back towards Henry. "It is only a matter of time, my old friend. The others are coming. Wolsey is your only hope." Thomas then headed into the shadows. Henry was stunned by what he had just heard. "Others! You mean to tell me that this nightmare is not over!"

Keith Coy

There was a creepy silence in the room. Nothing could be heard. Not even the servants shuffling about outside. Henry, still stunned by just looked around the room. He had almost decided to give up when suddenly Catherine of Aragon appeared again. "Oh no; not again. What is it this time?" He said.

Catherine moved into the light, the bloodstain like tear tracks on her face glowing. "Henry, you say you are innocent yet you have committed an act of such horrific proportions that words cannot begin to describe it" She said. Henry was not sure what it was his former wife was telling him. Catherine turned to the shadows. "You may enter into the room my dear." Henry stared into the shadows not certain of who was going to come out this time. Then a young girl appeared. She had a rough look about her; her clothes all ragged and tattered. Her head slightly tilted on one side. She had black rings around her eyes and she had no shoes on her feet. Henry was horrified by what he

The Ghosts of Henry VIII

was seeing. "Who is she?" He asked. Catherine didn't answer. "Who are you?" He asked the girl. The girl just stared at him.

"She will not answer you, she cannot" Catherine said, moving to stand next to the child. "You had her hanged" Henry looked shocked at her. "I did not!" Catherine stepped forward. "Yes you did, just look at her neck!" Henry averted his eyes and looked at the table. "Look at it, you fool, look at the poor girl's neck!" screamed Catherine as she moved nearer the table. Henry looked up at the young girl's neck. There he saw a big dark ring with black and purple all around where he could see. Catherine leant on the table. "In life her name was Alice Glaston and she lived in Much Wenlock where she had an easy life until you signed her execution order this year, the year of our Lord 1546. She was innocent. Just trying to get by. But one misfortune and you snuffed her out." Henry looked at the girl and began to tremble. "I had no idea, I swear to

Keith Coy

you; no idea. I would have spared you! Pray forgive me" The girl just stood there staring, her eyes shining in the candle light. Catherine went back to the girl and took her hand. "Forgiveness will be yours if you repent Henry." The two turned and headed towards the same shadow Thomas More did. Catherine turned around again. "On the eve before Christmas, an old courtier will come before you and you can see what happens if you do not repent." Then she and the girl disappeared into the shadows leaving Henry dumbfounded.

The Ghosts of Henry VIII

V

Catherine of Aragon's words seemed to have stuck with Henry as did the image of Alice because he ordered Thomas and Stephen to look into what happened in Much Wenlock. Which they did and what they learnt terrified them as much as if they had had their ghostly visits. In the hall of records, Stephen was busy looking over some papers when Thomas entered. "Why would the King order us to look into the executions of a small village? Surely the affairs of the villagers are that of the local sheriff and magistrate?" He asked. Stephen looked up from the paper he was looking at. "It is not our place to question the King or his reasoning for this investigation." He replied.

Some time had passed and the two priests were about to give up and call it a day when Stephen found something. "Good grief!" He cried, "Thomas; have a look at this!" Thomas turned and looked over Stephen's shoulder at the paper in his hand. Thomas felt a strange feeling in his stomach. "Why would the King allow something like this to happen?" He asked; Stephen shook his head. "I have not got an idea"

The two priests made their way back to Whitehall as quickly as they could. Racing down the galleries and corridors to reach Henry who was sitting in his privy library watching some birds. The two priests entered the library and almost fell over each other. Henry turned to see what all the commotion was.

"What is this all about?" He asked as the priests picked themselves up off the floor. Stephen stepped forward albeit unsteady on his feet. "We found some most distress in that investigation of the village you ordered" He said. Henry motioned the priests to sit down which they did. "What did you uncover?" Stephen struggled to find the words. "Majesty, earlier this year, you signed the execution order of a young girl named Alice Glaston." He said with a stutter. Henry tried to look shocked, not letting on that he already knew this. "What was her crime?" Stephen stuttered again. "Witchcraft, Sire!" Henry looked at both priests and stared out of the window again.

"I must have been tricked into signing it. Or my signature was forged. As for the charge, nonsense." He grumbled. Thomas looked surprised to hear this. "But Sire…" He began but Henry cut him off, "Nonsense I say. My enemies have been trying this for some time now. Found out whom and have my secretary arrested for treason. Go!" The two priests quickly fled the room.

Once outside and the door was shut, Stephen turned to Thomas. "What are we going to do?" Thomas shook his head. "I know not but one thing I do know. We are not arresting the poor innocent secretary."

Keith Coy

The next day, the eve before Christmas Eve, everyone was getting all excited. People were singing and being very happy indeed. Except for Thomas and Stephen who were more on edge than ever. Henry was known for erratic behaviour and notorious mind swings but it seemed that something had gotten him acting more stranger than usual. Sure Henry was prone to violent outbursts and sudden anger sessions but this was unusual. And they were about to find out why. That afternoon, Henry summoned the two priests to his privy apartments for a glass of wine and to discuss the festive period. It was tradition in the sixteenth century that from the day before Christmas Eve to Plough Monday all works and matters of state be suspended and all attention was focused on the Yuletide.

The priests entered the privy apartments and Henry offered them a glass of wine. "Gentlemen, I have been tough recently but thankfully it is nearly Christmas and I feel that until Plough Monday, we should just enjoy ourselves. After all, it is time when all men come together and celebrate the birth of our Lord. Here is to your health." Henry said and he raised a glass followed by the two priests raising theirs. "To your own good health and long may you continue to reign." Said Thomas while Stephen nodded in agreement.

The three of them seemed to enjoy the afternoon of drinking and chatting, that Henry completely forgot what Catherine of Aragon said about the Eve before Christmas and something about an old courtier. As the sunlight began to fade, the three men looked out of the window and watched as the snow outside came down heavily. Then out of the brief silence came a sorrowful moan.

"Gardiner, what are you moaning for?" Asked Henry without looking at him. Stephen looked surprised by this. "I am not, Your Majesty." He said as the moaning sound continued. Both Henry and Stephen looked at Thomas who shook his head. But before he could answer, the sound of the door behind them opened and they all turned round. They watched as the door slowly opened and the sound of chains being dragged along the floor could be heard.

The door finally swung open and the sounds of moaning and dragging chains grew louder, fear began to grip the three men. Henry went to call out but before he could, there appeared a sight that Henry thought he would never see again. A sight he had not seen since 1521. For standing there in the doorway, in chains that looked completely heavy was the Duke of Buckingham, Edward Stafford.

"I would say it is nice to see you again," Edward said as he stepped into the room and stopped only the remainder of the chains. "But I would be lying, not after what we both did." Henry almost fell back into his chair but was assisted by the two priests who both looked at each other and then at the sight before them. Thomas was at a loss to explain what

The Ghosts of Henry VIII

he was seeing. It was not possible. Yet here he stood. Edward looked straight at Henry. "Heed me Henry, for I do not have long. The powers above have agreed to let me come to you this evening because the Cardinal persuaded them." He said; the chains behind began to move. "You are at great peril of suffering my fate if you do not repent." Henry glared at Edward, "Not you as well. And why are you in those chains?" He said pointing to the chains around Edward. The chains began to move again this time pulling Edward backwards. "When I was executed in the year of our Lord 1521, I never repented. Never sought forgiveness. My desire to live cost me my eternal rest. I shall never know peace because I refused to repent. I shall never know paradise. Forever doomed to walk this earth in chains." The chains pulled Edward some more until he was standing in the doorway again. "I beseech you Henry; do not suffer the fate I am. Seek out the cardinal and repent. You sought forgiveness but you must now repent. Repent!" And then as if someone had given the chains a large tug, Edward was pulled out of the doorway and back into the darkness. The door slowly closed again. Edward's voice called out again. "Repent, you must repent!"

There was an uncomfortable silence in the room shortly after. Nobody didn't know what to say or what they had just heard. Thomas poured everyone a glass of wine and they drank in silence. Thomas told the others that he needed to dismiss himself briefly and left the room. Henry told Stephen to fetch some food. Stephen left the room and Henry was alone.

Henry sat in the room staring at the door which was closed again. He was having trouble making sense of the events that were taking place. Why now? Why me? Henry shook his head and shrugged it off. He took a swig of wine and looked out of the window again but this time instead of snow, he saw the images of Catherine of Aragon and Alice staring back out.

The Ghosts of Henry VIII

"Why is this happening to me?" He whimpered. Catherine and Alice just stared back. "Pray answer, why?" Catherine's image then manifested into the room while Alice remained in the window. "It is simple, you must repent. Save yourself from the darkness. You heard Buckingham, seek out Wolsey." She said.

The doors behind him opened and the two priests and some servants entered followed by some trays of food. Henry looked at them all briefly before turning back to the window but the images of Catherine and Alice were gone.

The afternoon turned into evening and the food was gone. Henry took a little nap while Thomas and Stephen tried to work out the afternoon's activity. After a lengthy discussion, they decided that it was best to forget for the time being and pick it up again after Christmas.

Henry woke from his nap and found only Stephen sitting in the room. "Cramner giving his sermon already?" He asked but Stephen shook his head. "No Sire, just in the next room working on his sermon for midnight mass tomorrow." Henry told Stephen that he was pleased to hear it. "I think it is the best time to send for more wine." Henry said, picking his goblet and seeing it empty.

Stephen called for a servant and told him to fetch more jugs of wine. Then he turned back to Henry. "Bit of an odd occurrence this afternoon, Sire." He said. Henry snarled. "Aye but I still think someone is trying to have a jest with me." He said as he pulled his leg onto a stall. "It is in very poor taste and I will not have it" Stephen went to step forward but then he stood. Henry noticed this and it looked as though Stephen was frozen in time. "What is wrong with man?" He demanded but Stephen just stood there. Then his head flopped down, face towards the floor. "Gardiner?" Henry began to feel uneasy. "Cramner, get in here now!"

The Ghosts of Henry VIII

He called out. The air became all funny and then nothing.

The scene made Henry squirm slightly and where was Thomas? Then Henry heard Wolsey's voice. "Henry Tudor, why do you resist?" Henry heard exactly where the voice was coming from but he didn't believe it. It was coming from Stephen. Thomas rushed into the room just in time to see Stephen raised his head up. His eyes were shut tight. Then he opened them and bright yellow light emanated from the sockets. "I am trying to save you Henry. Your end is neigh and you must repent. Come seek me in the great hall. I am your hope." Both Henry and Thomas didn't know what to make of it all as they watched the light fade. Then Stephen's head flopped again but this time he fell to the floor with a crash causing guards to enter the room.

After a few minutes, Stephen came around; he explained how he felt and what had happened. Henry sat for

Keith Coy

```
a while thinking. I guess I have no
other options left.
```

VI

January 1547.

Christmas passed without any further hauntings; so much so that Henry thought that it might be safe to resume his normal activities. Except he was wrong in more ways than one.

One evening on 10th January, Henry was sitting in his privy apartments reading all the reports and warrants and petitions that had arrived on his desk since the 7th January. He had his secretary put them into piles. Do something, ignore and be destroyed. He came across a letter about a dispute of some gold that was discovered on some land outside of Staines and he ordered his secretary to write a letter stating that he would have the gold and that the dispute would be settled by the men or else.

Thomas and Stephen entered the room. Henry dismissed his secretary for the evening. "Have that letter sent out by the morrow!" Henry said as Thomas and Stephen stepped aside to let the secretary pass. Once the door was closed, Thomas sat down while Stephen poured some wine. "I must say Sire you are looking much better since the incident just before Christmas." Thomas as he was handed a goblet of wine. Henry smiled. "I am but what about you, Gardiner?" Stephen sat down. "I am well but that night is forever in my mind." He said.

Henry took a swig of wine and placed the goblet on the table next to him. "Heed me Gardiner, what has happened here recently was nothing to speak of lightly nor to be spoken of outside this room." Henry said, his eyes darting between Thomas and Stephen. Thomas simply took a swig of wine from his goblet. "Besides that is all over now and we have matters to attend to. How fares the trial of that leech Thomas Howard?"

The Ghosts of Henry VIII

"Norfolk is putting up a fight saying that he is the victim and that his family has gotten it in for him." Said Thomas sitting back in his chair, "Claims that he was being used to advance others around him." Henry roared with laughter. "Does he think me a fool?" He chortled, "Twas he who pushed those nieces of his on me. Twas he who had me execute my loyal and faithful servants More and Cromwell. Twas he who had me banish my most cherished friend and advisor Wolsey." Henry picked up his goblet, "No, Howard is the traitor. Ambitions above his own station. Ideas of grandeur. Pushing his agendas on me. No gentlemen, he goes to the scaffolding. Even if he is dragged onto it."

After a lengthy discussion of other things as well, the trio decided to go for a walk. Henry was slower now because of his leg. As he walked, holding onto his staff for supporting; he could not help but think about his younger days and what it was like to be the most sporting

King of England. He completely ignored his surroundings and was tuned out of hearing the conversation of Thomas and Stephen. Bliss.

After a while Henry stopped and sat down on a nearby gallery windowsill. He gently rubbed his leg. Thomas went to send Stephen to fetch some water but Henry said that he would be fine. "Stop fussing Cranmer, I will be fine after a little rest. Damn it man, you are like an old lady!" Henry snapped. It was about to be clear that he would regret mentioning an old lady.

Thomas and Stephen went off to check if the King's apartments were nearby after the walk. The evening was slowly darkening into night and the torch lighters relit the torches both inside and outside. Henry watched as the workers slowly disappeared from view. Then he turned to see if the priests were on their way back with support for him. Then he saw her.

The Ghosts of Henry VIII

Standing there just out of the shadows, stood his grandmother; Lady Margaret Beaufort. Her stern face and angry eyes fixed on Henry. Henry tried to get to his feet but he could not, having been sitting too long. Margaret moved forward. Her headdress which glistened with gold and jewels was dull. Henry watched as she approached and then stopped short of him. Her eyes clearer now and the anger was visible to see. Henry tried to speak but he had lost his voice.

"Well what do you have to say for yourself?" Margaret said, her voice sounded with fury. Henry just could not bring himself to speak. It seemed that as it was when she was alive, he was terrified of his grandmother. All he could do was stutter. Margaret shook her head.

"Very well, listen! You have doomed everything that I had envisioned for this family. Everything your father has worked hard to achieve and secure. He is furious and I do not blame him. You have blackened the name Henry. And what is worst you have committed sin after sin. I did not bring you up to have such beliefs. Nor did I teach you to be arrogant to others. And when I cause you to have a little accident on your horse, what do you do? Chop your friends' heads off. I am disappointed in you. I had such hopes that you continue the work that your father and I started; instead, you throw away your marriage to a good woman for a power grabber. Doomed the souls of your people by breaking away from Rome and I think you know about poor Alice." Margaret glared at her grandson. "Now when given a chance to repent, you refuse. How dare you. You will seek out Cardinal Wolsey and beg him for redemption. Or so help me, I will haunt you to your very end." Margaret stepped back, raised her arms and disappeared in a veil of white light. "I mean it Henry."

Henry sat there in complete shock at what he had just heard. He knew that he was out of options and

The Ghosts of Henry VIII

now the hauntings were starting again and what did his grandmother mean to beg for redemption when the other ghosts had told him that they were trying to save his soul. After a while, Henry got to his feet and began to walk back to his apartments. As he slowly limbed back, Thomas and Stephen returned and rushed to assist him but Henry simply batted their hands away.

"We are nearly there, Majesty." Said Thomas as they turned a corner. Henry saw the doors to his apartments but he stopped for a bit. And it would be the last time he stepped outside of his apartments; for at that moment, there was a small whistling sound coming down the corridor followed by a voice calling his name. "Henry!" The voice called. Thomas and Stephen looked around holding their crucifixes in the air. "Henry!" The voice sounded like it was getting closer.

Then the torches dimed as if they were low on the fuel that lit them. The whistling sound continued. Then the voice sounded again, this time it was a shout making all three men jump. "Henry!"

    Then there was a strange white plume of smoke raising up from the ground followed by a loud bang that sounded like cannon fire. Thomas and Stephen fell backwards on the ground while Henry held onto his staff, the smoke cleared revealing Henry's father standing there. And he glared angrily at Henry while the two priests looked shocked and scared.

VII

Henry VII stared at Henry VIII with such anger that it almost looked like he was about to bust a blood vessel if he was still alive. Both father and son just stared at each other. The tension was thick, neither one of them spoke. Then Henry VII stepped forward and with a wave of his hand; he knocked out Thomas and Stephen. Both priests fell back and avoided hitting their heads on the cobbles.

"Why have you done that to my loyal men?" Henry VIII asked, Henry VII stopped in front of him. "We need to have a chat and I do not want them to hear what I have to say." Henry VII said. Henry VIII staggered but continued to hold onto his staff. "I do not wish to speak," He said, "I wish to go to my apartments and rest." Henry VII glared at his son with wide eyes. "Very well then you shall heed me to what I have to say."

Keith Coy

Henry VII moved closer to his son with a pale light glowing all around him. Unlike the lights of the other ghosts, this light was of a purple colour but it was so pale that Henry VIII could only see it when his father got closer to him. The two were almost in each other's face and then Henry VII spoke.

"When I won the field at Bosworth Field in the year of our Lord 1485 and claimed the crown and the throne in the name of Tudor, I had hopes of a dynasty that would live on down the ages. A dynasty that people would say; Henry Tudor built this dynasty. His descendants made this country. I had hoped that my sons would help create this vision for the future and move the country away from the wars of the Plantagenets and their family feuding. But fate intervened and one of my sons was cruelly taken from me. My hopes began to fade. But then I realised that my other son who was destined to be King after me would continue my legacy."

The Ghosts of Henry VIII

Henry VIII gasped, "I did, I have!" Henry VII shook his head. "No, have not!" Henry VII walked over to a nearby window. "You have ruined everything I achieved and worked for by your own ambitions, your greed. You allowed men to rule you instead of you ruling them." He turned to face his son again.

"I have watched as you have turned everything into you. You completely ignored the advice I gave you. You wanted more than you should have. You broke Rome all because you could not get your own way."

Henry VIII began to grow angry. "But at the time, I had no son. I nearly died and there would have been no male heir to continue your dynasty." He barked, "Only a daughter. And we know what happened the last time that..." Henry VII cut him off.

"Mary might have been different to Matilda. She might have been a good Queen and she would still be a ruling member of the House Tudor. But you never gave her a chance. Cast her and Catherine of Aragon aside because Norfolk told you to. You married a woman who was above her own station, power grabbing. And not to mention the other things you have done. I am disappointed in you. You have failed to grasp simple kingsmanship."

The two Kings stood face to face like they were about to draw swords and launch into a duel. An uncomfortable silence fell between them. A bell somewhere chimed the hour. Henry VII looked at his son and shook his head again. "Look to the Cardinal and repent Henry. Your time is growing shorter. Look for me no more until you have repented. Fare you well." The strange white plume of smoke appeared to rise up from the ground again only this time there was no loud cannon like bang just a small pop. When it cleared Henry VII was gone. Henry VIII looked down at the two priests who were now coming round again. "Ah to hell with it, I will seek out Wolsey then!" He then

The Ghosts of Henry VIII

hobbled towards his apartments.
Thomas and Stephen rose to the feet
and ran after him.

VIII

Henry never sent to the priests the next day nor did he grant access to him. He sat in his apartments looking over some papers, thinking about the last few weeks and what had been happening. He began to feel his life slowly fading. He was so deep in thought that he didn't realise that the surgeon had come to see to his leg until a sharp pain caught his attention.

"Watch what you are doing man!" Cried Henry as he winced in pain, "You are working on the leg of your King not some pox ridden serf!" The surgeon swapped knives and looked up at Henry. "I am sorry Majesty, I know that you hate this, so I will make it quick." He said as he placed a bowl under the leg. "Aye and see that you are careful." The surgeon nodded. "I will"

Henry went back to his thoughts and he stared up at a painting on the

The Ghosts of Henry VIII

wall. It was an ideal scene of sorts not that Henry could make out what it was but he focused on it while the surgeon worked on his leg. After a few minutes, the scene began to change. Henry tried to sit forward but he couldn't. His eyes widened as the image of little Alice appeared in the painting. Her sad face staring down at him. Henry felt the fear creep into him like a snake slithering through the grass of a field. He slowly shook his head. He went to say something but the surgeon again caught attention. This time tying some bandages. The surgeon stood up. "All done." He said, Henry glared at him. "Get Out!"

That afternoon, Henry had the guards take him to his privy library and told them to leave him until supper time. The guards departed. Henry made sure he was alone before he called out. "Alright Wolsey, you win. I give up." There was a small gust of wind blowing around and Wolsey appeared. The red glow around dimed. "You say you give up but are you going to repent?" He asked as he came into view. Henry nodded. "Aye."

Wolsey walked over to Henry before looking around. "So this is what has become of York Place? Turned into a Palace. And What have you done with my Palace at Hampton Court? Oh that is it, you enlarged it." He said, fixing his cold icy stare on Henry again. "The powers above have deemed you to be too dark Henry. Too dark and too unstable but I convinced them that I can save you." Henry stared back. "Was it really necessary to send the others and my father?" Wolsey nodded.

Thomas and Stephen could be heard on the other side of the door trying to plead for an audience with Henry but he simply ignored them. Wolsey looked at the door as if though he could see through. "Oh how those two have failed you on a scale that you will never know." He said. Then he turned back to Henry. "The time of your end is neigh Henry, repent and you will be saved." Henry

The Ghosts of Henry VIII

got annoyed. "I said I will." He looked into the room and saw Catherine of Aragon, Alice, Thomas More and a group of monks standing there.

"Henry Tudor, King of England, Ireland and France. Eighth King of that name, you are a sinner of great proportions. You have committed acts so unspeakable; you have declared too dark. Your soul has become a desired prize. Will you repent your sins and come back to the light?"

"Aye"

"Will you repent for your deeds done to the church in the name of greed?"

"Aye"

"Will you repent for breaking your vows to Catherine of Aragon?"

"Aye"

"Will you repent for what you did to your friends?"

Keith Coy

"Aye."

"Will you repent for what you did to this poor child?"

"Aye and I am sorry!"

A gust of wind blew up and Catherine, Alice and Thomas disappeared. Henry looked around and saw that Wolsey was standing. Not in a red glow or pale but as he did in life. "Henry Tudor, I hereby accept your penance and absorb you. You are saved." Wolsey disappeared. Henry gave a sigh of relief. It was over. Henry looked into the room and saw that the monks were still standing. "Wolsey, monks?"

IX

27th/28th January 1547.

Eventually Henry became far too ill and took to his bed. Thomas and Stephen were finally allowed access to him and plans were being made for the succession though nobody dared to mention that Henry was dying. Thomas knew different though. He summoned everyone of importance to the royal bedchambers.

"Now before I send for Prince Edward, I just want to say that the King does not have long left. I feel it is time for us to say goodbye. I will admit you all momentarily and then I will send for the Prince. But for one last time, God save the King!"

"God save the King!"

In his bedchamber, Henry heard the commotion outside. God save the

King. That he did, more times than I deserved. Thankfully so did Wolsey.

The door opened and the court poured in and paid compliments to Henry before they were ushered into a nearby chamber. Henry could hear the sobbing but he began to slip in and out of consciousness. He must have passed out because when he came to, Prince Edward was standing there.

"Edward, my lad!" Henry said softly, "You will soon be King and I want you to promise that you will be a good and true King. Learn from my mistakes. Rule with compassion and above all rule in the name of God."

Edward shed a small tear. "Yes Father and I will bear many a son too." Henry gave a small smile. "There will be plenty of time for that decision when you are older. Be kind to your sisters and your stepmother. Look after them well. Remember, I will be watching." Edward nodded. "Good lad, ok off you go."

The Ghosts of Henry VIII

Thomas escorted Edward out of the chamber and Henry was left alone. He stared vacantly around the room. Then he noticed the group of monks. He tried to call out but instead he passed out.

He could hear Thomas asking if he accepted someone or something but he simply could not respond. Instead he squeezed Thomas' hand. "Monks, Monks, Monks"

Thomas leaned in and checked on Henry. He turned round, his face pale.

The King is dead, Long Live the King!

www.ingramcontent.com/pod-product-compliance
Lightning Source LLC
Chambersburg PA
CBHW070550090426
42735CB00013B/3133